table of contents

dips & spreads

dressings

sauces

soups

vitamix techniques

important safeguards

⚠WARNING: To avoid the risk of serious injury when using your Vitamix® Blender, basic safety precautions should be followed including the following.

READ ALL INSTRUCTIONS, SAFEGUARDS AND WARNINGS BEFORE OPERATING BLENDER.

1. Read all instructions.

2. Not intended for use by or near children or persons with reduced physical, sensory, or mental capabilities or lack of experience and knowledge. Close supervision is necessary when any appliance is used by or near children or incapacitated persons.

3. To protect against risk of electrical shock do not put blender base in water or other liquid.

4. Unplug from outlet when not in use, before putting on or taking off parts, and before cleaning.

5. Avoid contacting moving parts.

6. Do not operate any appliance with a damaged cord or plug or after the appliance malfunctions, or is dropped or damaged in any manner. Call Vitamix Customer Service 800-848-2649 or 440-235-4840 or email service@vitamix.com at once for examination, repair, replacement, or electrical or mechanical adjustment. If purchased outside the U.S.A. or Canada, contact your local Vitamix dealer.

7. Alteration or modification of any part of the blender base or container including the use of any part or parts that are not genuine authorized Vitamix parts may cause fire, electric shock or injury.

8. The use of attachments not expressly authorized or sold by Vitamix for use with this blender, including canning jars, may cause fire, electric shock or injury.

9. Do not use outdoors.

10. Do not let cord hang over edge of table or counter.

11. Do not let cord contact hot surface, including the stove.

12. Keep hands and utensils out of container while blending to reduce the risk of severe injury to persons or damage to the blender. A rubber scraper or spatula may be used but only when the Vitamix blender is not running.

13. The tamper provided must be used only when the main part of the lid is in place.

14. Blades are sharp. Handle or remove blade and blade assembly from the container with extreme care to avoid injury. To reduce the risk of injury, never place a blade assembly on the motor base unless assembled to the Vitamix container.

15. Do not leave foreign objects in container such as spoons, forks, knives or the lid plug as this will damage the blades and other components when starting the machine and may cause injury.

16. Never attempt to operate with damaged blades.

17. Always operate blender with lid and lid plug firmly in place. The lid plug should only be removed when adding ingredients and when using the tamper.

18. When blending hot liquids or ingredients use caution; spray or escaping steam may cause scalding and burns. Do not fill container to the maximum capacity. Always begin processing on the lowest speed setting - variable speed 1. Keep hands and other exposed skin away from the lid opening to prevent possible burns.

19. When making nut butters or oil based foods, do not process for more than one minute after the mixture starts to circulate in the container. Processing for longer periods can cause dangerous overheating.

SAVE THESE INSTRUCTIONS

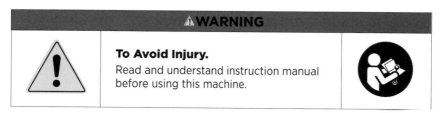

⚠WARNING	
To Avoid Injury. Read and understand instruction manual before using this machine.	

IMPORTANT INSTRUCTIONS FOR SAFE USE

This product is intended for HOUSEHOLD USE ONLY and is not intended to be used for commercial purposes.

Do not leave your Vitamix blender unattended when operating.

Any repair, servicing, or the replacement of parts, must be performed by Vitamix or an authorized service representative.

⚠WARNING
Electrical Shock Hazard. Use grounded outlet only. **DO NOT** remove ground. **DO NOT** use an adapter. **DO NOT** use an extension cord. **Failure to follow instructions can cause death or electrical shock.**

NOTICE: FAILURE TO FOLLOW ANY OF THE IMPORTANT SAFEGUARDS AND THE IMPORTANT INSTRUCTIONS FOR SAFE USE IS A <u>MISUSE</u> OF YOUR VITAMIX BLENDER THAT CAN VOID YOUR WARRANTY AND CREATE THE RISK OF SERIOUS INJURY.

WET BLADE CONTAINER

Designed for processing liquids including juice, frozen mixtures, sauces, soups, purees, batters, and for wet chopping.

1. Make sure that the Variable Speed Dial is set to 1.

2. Load the container before placing it on the motor base. Place liquids and soft foods in the container first, solid items and ice last. Although not necessary for blending, you may want to cut or break food into smaller pieces for more precise measuring of ingredients.

3. Securely fasten the 2-part lid. Always use the complete 2-part lid when blending (unless the tamper is inserted through the lid plug opening). Especially when blending hot ingredients, make sure the lid is securely latched.

4. With the motor off, set the wet blade container on the motor base by aligning it over the centering pad. Do not ever attempt to put a container on an operating motor base or to operate a motor base without a container properly in place.

5. Start with the High/Variable Switch in the Variable (⊿) position. Always start your machine on variable speed 1. Activate the machine by turning the On/Off Switch to On (|) then slowly increase to the desired speed. Your container will shift and get into an aligned position.

6. **Take proper care when handling and processing hot ingredients and making hot soups and sauces.**

⚠CAUTION		
	Never Start on Speeds Above 1 with Hot Liquids to Avoid Possible Burns. Use Caution; escaping steam or splashes may scald. Lock the lid. This will prevent expansion from affecting the position of the lid when the machine is turned on. Start on Variable 1, slowly increase to 10.	

7. Due to the machine's speed, processing times are much quicker than standard appliances. Until you are accustomed to the machine, count your time carefully to avoid over processing.

8. After turning the machine off, wait until the blades completely stop before removing the lid or container from the motor base.

DRY BLADE CONTAINER

If purchased, your dry blade container should only be used for hard, dry materials, such as grain, and for kneading dough.

1. Make sure that the Variable Speed Dial is set to 1.

2. Securely fasten the 2-part lid. Always use the complete 2-part lid when blending (unless the tamper is inserted through the lid plug opening).

3. With the motor off, set the dry blade container on the motor base by aligning it over the centering pad. Do not ever attempt to put a container on an operating motor base or to operate a motor base without a container properly in place.

4. Start with the High/Variable Switch in the Variable (△) position. Always start your machine on variable speed 1. Activate the machine by turning the On/Off Switch to On (|) then slowly increase to the desired speed. Your container will shift and get into an aligned position.

5. After turning the machine off, wait until the blades completely stop before removing the lid or container from the motor base.

6. Due to the machine's speed, processing times are much quicker than standard appliances. Until you are accustomed to the machine, count your time carefully to avoid over processing.

7. Grinding dry material for more than two minutes could damage your machine. Regular use may result in cosmetic marring of the container and cause the blades to become dull over time.

8. Grinding some herbs may release volatile oils, causing the container to discolor permanently. Others have strong odors that may linger in the container, affecting the flavour of other foods. The grinding of some herbs and spices may also cause the blade to dull over time, or the container to crack.

notes

BLENDING

This may be the most enjoyable feature of your Vitamix®. The precision engineering of the Vitamix machine makes it possible to achieve the best blended recipes. Whether you're making creamy smoothies, creating milk substitutes, mixing drinks or blending butters and batters, the Vitamix machine makes it all so easy. The secret's in the Variable Speed Dial. It allows you to control the blades and therefore provides versatility at various blending speeds. You can now prepare foods in a totally new and inventive way.

BLENDING

TRIPLE BERRY SMOOTHIE

preparation: 10 minutes • processing: 1 minute • yield: 1 1/2 cups (360 ml)

1/2 cup (120 ml) water

1/4 cup (60 g) low fat vanilla yogurt

1/2 cup (75 g) frozen unsweetened strawberries

1/2 cup (80 g) frozen unsweetened blueberries

1/2 cup (70 g) frozen unsweetened raspberries

1. Place all ingredients into the Vitamix container in the order listed and secure lid.

2. Select Variable 1.

3. Turn machine on and slowly increase speed to Variable 10, then to High.

4. Blend for 1 minute or until desired consistency is reached.

NOTE: For best results, allow frozen fruit to thaw at room temperature 5 minutes before blending.

Per Recipe: 165 Cal (9% from Fat, 11% from Protein, 80% from Carb); 5 g Protein; 2 g Tot Fat; 1 g Sat Fat; 36 g Carb; 9 g Fiber; 24 g Sugar; 45 mg Sodium; 3 mg Cholesterol

FROZEN STRAWBERRY GRAPE JUICE

preparation: 10 minutes • processing: 40-45 seconds • yield: 2 1/2 cups (600 ml)

1 cup (150 g) green grapes

1 cup (150 g) red grapes

1 cup (150 g) frozen unsweetened strawberries

1/2 cup (120 ml) ice cubes

1. Place all ingredients into the Vitamix container in the order listed and secure lid.

2. Select Variable 1.

3. Turn machine on and slowly increase speed to Variable 10, then to High.

4. Blend for 40 to 45 seconds or until desired consistency is reached.

Per 1 Cup (240 ml) Serving: 119 Cal (2% from Fat, 4% from Protein, 94% from Carb); 1 g Protein; 0 g Tot Fat; 0 g Sat Fat; 31 g Carb; 3 g Fiber; 24 g Sugar; 4 mg Sodium; 0 mg Cholesterol

BASIC MILKSHAKE AND
SUGGESTED FLAVOR ADD-INS

preparation: 10 minutes • processing: 15-20 seconds • yield: 2 cups (480 ml)

1/4 cup (60 ml) milk

1 teaspoon vanilla extract

2 cups (264 g)
vanilla ice cream

**We suggest adding any
of the following items for
a tasty twist on tradition:**

2 Tablespoons (44 g)
chocolate milk powder

1/2 cup (62 g) raspberries

1/2 cup (74 g) blueberries

4 medium strawberries

2 chocolate
sandwich cookies

1 Tablespoon jam

1 Tablespoon chocolate
hazelnut spread

1 teaspoon honey

1/2 cup (15 g) crunch
cereal or granola

2 Tablespoons (39 g)
maple syrup

1. Place all ingredients and desired add-ins into the Vitamix container in the order listed and secure lid.

2. Select Variable 1.

3. Turn machine on and slowly increase speed to Variable 10, then to High.

4. Blend for 15 to 20 seconds or until desired consistency is reached.

Per 1 Cup (240 ml) Serving (without add-ins): 313 Cal (48% from Fat, 8% from Protein, 45% from Carb); 6 g Protein; 17 g Tot Fat; 10 g Sat Fat; 36 g Carb; 1 g Fiber; 32 g Sugar; 127 mg Sodium; 66 mg Cholesterol

blending

FROZEN WHISKY SOUR

preparation: 10 minutes • processing: 30 seconds • yield: 3 1/4 cups (780 ml)

6 ounces (180 ml) bourbon

2 lemons, peeled, halved

1 medium orange, peeled, halved

1/4 cup (50 g) sugar

3 cups (720 ml) ice cubes

1. Place all ingredients into the Vitamix container in the order listed and secure lid.

2. Select Variable 1.

3. Turn machine on and slowly increase speed to Variable 8.

4. Blend for 30 seconds or until desired consistency is reached.

Per 1 Cup (240 ml) Serving: 223 Cal (2% from Fat, 3% from Protein, 95% from Carb); 1 g Protein; 0 g Tot Fat; 0 g Sat Fat; 25 g Carb; 2 g Fiber; 20 g Sugar; 2 mg Sodium; 0 mg Cholesterol

STRAWBERRY DAIQUIRI

preparation: 10 minutes • processing: 40 seconds • yield: 2 1/2 cups (600 ml)

2 ounces (60 ml) light rum

1 ounce (30 ml) Grand Marnier or triple sec

2 Tablespoons (30 ml) sweetened lime juice

2 Tablespoons (25 g) sugar

4-6 large ripe fresh strawberries, hulled

1 cup (150 g) frozen unsweetened strawberries

1 1/2 cups (360 ml) ice cubes

1. Place all ingredients into the Vitamix container in the order listed and secure lid.

2. Select Variable 1.

3. Turn machine on and slowly increase speed to Variable 10, then to High.

4. Blend for 40 seconds or until desired consistency is reached.

Per 1 Cup (240 ml) Serving: 176 Cal (1% from Fat, 2% from Protein, 97% from Carb); 1 g Protein; 0 g Tot Fat; 0 g Sat Fat; 26 g Carb; 2 g Fiber; 20 g Sugar; 3 mg Sodium; 0 mg Cholesterol

WHOLE FRUIT MARGARITA

preparation: 15 minutes • processing: 45 seconds • yield: 6 cups (1.4 l)

1/4 cup (60 ml) water

6 ounces (180 ml) tequila

2 ounces (60 ml) Grand Marnier or triple sec

1 medium orange, peeled, halved

1 lime, peeled, halved

1 lemon, peeled, halved

6 Tablespoons (75 g) sugar

6 cups (1.4 l) ice cubes

1. Place all ingredients into the Vitamix container in the order listed and secure lid.

2. Select Variable 1.

3. Turn machine on and slowly increase speed to Variable 10, then to High.

4. Blend for 45 seconds or until desired consistency is reached.

5. Pour into salt-rimmed margarita glasses.

NOTE: For a fun variation, serve in sugar-rimmed margarita glasses.

Per 1 Cup (240 ml) Serving: 174 Cal (1% from Fat, 2% from Protein, 97% from Carb); 0 g Protein; 0 g Tot Fat; 0 g Sat Fat; 22 g Carb; 1 g Fiber; 20 g Sugar; 2 mg Sodium; 0 mg Cholesterol

CAPPUCCINO

preparation: 10 minutes • processing: 30 seconds • yield: 1 1/4 cups (300 ml)

3/4 cup (180 ml) hot milk

1 Tablespoon white chocolate chips

1 teaspoon instant espresso powder

1 teaspoon vanilla extract

1. Place all ingredients into the Vitamix container in the order listed and secure lid.

2. Select Variable 1.

3. Turn machine on and slowly increase speed to Variable 8.

4. Blend for 30 seconds or until desired consistency is reached.

NOTE: For a frozen version, use 1 cup (240 ml) cold milk, add 1/2 cup (120 ml) ice cubes, and increase espresso powder to 2 teaspoons. Blend on Variable 8 for 30 seconds.

Per Recipe: 182 Cal (49% from Fat, 15% from Protein, 36% from Carb); 7 g Protein; 9 g Tot Fat; 5 g Sat Fat; 15 g Carb; 0 g Fiber; 16 g Sugar; 83 mg Sodium; 19 mg Cholesterol

VANILLA COFFEE FRAPPÉ

preparation: 10 minutes • processing: 30 seconds • yield: 4 cups (960 ml)

3/4 cup (180 ml) double-strength coffee or espresso, cooled

1 cup (240 ml) milk

3 Tablespoons (45 ml) vanilla syrup

1 1/2 teaspoons vanilla extract

1 1/2 cups (360 ml) ice cubes

1. Place all ingredients into the Vitamix container in the order listed and secure lid.

2. Select Variable 1.

3. Turn machine on and slowly increase speed to Variable 8.

4. Blend for 30 seconds or until desired consistency is reached.

NOTE: Vanilla syrup can be found in the coffee section of most grocery stores.

Per 1 Cup (240 ml) Serving: 82 Cal (29% from Fat, 11% from Protein, 60% from Carb); 2 g Protein; 2 g Tot Fat; 1 g Sat Fat; 11 g Carb; 0 g Fiber; 11 g Sugar; 25 mg Sodium; 6 mg Cholesterol

GOING GREEN SMOOTHIE

preparation: 10 minutes • processing: 30 seconds • yield: 2 1/2 cups (600 ml)

1/2 cup (120 ml) water

1 cup (150 g) green grapes

1/2 cup (75 g) fresh
pineapple chunks

1/2 medium
banana, peeled

2 cups (60 g) fresh
spinach, lightly packed

1/2 cup (120 ml) ice cubes

1. Place all ingredients into the Vitamix container in the order listed and secure lid.

2. Select Variable 1.

3. Turn machine on and slowly increase speed to Variable 10, then to High.

4. Blend for 30 seconds or until desired consistency is reached.

NOTE: If using frozen pineapple, omit the ice cubes.

Per 1 Cup (240 ml) Serving: 87 Cal (3% from Fat, 6% from Protein, 91% from Carb); 2 g Protein; 0 g Tot Fat; 0 g Sat Fat; 22 g Carb; 2 g Fiber; 16 g Sugar; 22 mg Sodium; 0 mg Cholesterol

blending

WORLD'S BEST MALTED MILKSHAKE

preparation: 10 minutes • processing: 15-20 seconds • yield: 2 3/4 cups (660 ml)

1/4 cup (60 ml) milk

1/4 cup (60 ml)
chocolate syrup

1/4 cup (66 g)
malted milk powder

3 cups (396 g)
vanilla ice cream

1. Place all ingredients into the Vitamix container in the order listed and secure lid.

2. Select Variable 1.

3. Turn machine on and slowly increase speed to Variable 10, then to High.

4. Blend for 15 to 20 seconds, using the tamper to press the ingredients into the blades.

Per 1 Cup (240 ml) Serving: 439 Cal (37% from Fat, 8% from Protein, 56% from Carb); 9 g Protein; 18 g Tot Fat; 11 g Sat Fat; 63 g Carb; 2 g Fiber; 53 g Sugar; 244 mg Sodium; 72 mg Cholesterol

FRUIT SALAD SMOOTHIE

preparation: 15 minutes • processing: 30-40 seconds • yield: 3 cups (720 ml)

1/2 cup (75 g)
green grapes

1 medium orange, peeled, halved

1/2-inch-thick (1.3 cm)
slice pineapple, core included, halved

1/2 cup (65 g) peeled and chopped cucumber

1 medium carrot,
4 ounces (114 g), halved

1/4 medium apple, seeded

2 cups (480 ml) ice cubes

1. Place all ingredients into the Vitamix container in the order listed and secure lid.

2. Select Variable 1.

3. Turn machine on and slowly increase speed to Variable 10, then to High.

4. Blend for 30 to 40 seconds, using the tamper to press the ingredients into the blades.

Per 1 Cup (240 ml) Serving: 65 Cal (3% from Fat, 6% from Protein, 92% from Carb); 1 g Protein; 0 g Tot Fat; 0 g Sat Fat; 17 g Carb; 2 g Fiber; 12 g Sugar; 11 mg Sodium; 0 mg Cholesterol

TASTES LIKE SUMMER GREEN SMOOTHIE

preparation: 10 minutes • processing: 30 seconds • yield: 2 3/4 cups (660 ml)

1/2 cup (120 ml) water

1 1/2 cups (225 g) green grapes

2 1/2 cups (75 g) fresh spinach leaves

1/2 cup (12 g) fresh basil leaves

1 Tablespoon fresh parsley leaves

1/2 orange, peeled

1 cup (165 g) fresh or frozen, thawed mango chunks

1/2-1 cup (120-240 ml) ice cubes

1. Place all ingredients into the Vitamix container in the order listed and secure lid.

2. Select Variable 1.

3. Turn machine on and slowly increase speed to Variable 10, then to High.

4. Blend for 30 seconds or until desired consistency is reached.

Per 1 Cup (240 ml) Serving: 126 Cal (3% from Fat, 7% from Protein, 90% from Carb); 2 g Protein; 1 g Tot Fat; 0 g Sat Fat; 32 g Carb; 4 g Fiber; 26 g Sugar; 27 mg Sodium; 0 mg Cholesterol

blending

SOY MILK

preparation: 8 hours • processing: 1 minute • cook time: 15 minutes • yield: 4 cups (960 ml) unstrained or 3 cups (720 ml) strained

1 cup (200 g) dried
soy beans

1 Tablespoon sugar

3 1/2 cups (840 ml) water

1. Clean dried soy beans and soak in water for 4 to 8 hours. Steam for about 15 minutes.

2. Drain soy beans and let cool. Measure 1 1/2 cups (258 g) cooked beans.

3. Place cooked beans, sugar, and water into the Vitamix container in the order listed and secure lid.

4. Select Variable 1.

5. Turn machine on and slowly increase speed to Variable 10, then to High.

6. Blend for 1 minute or until desired consistency is reached.

7. To obtain commercial-style soy milk, strain the milk through a nut milk bag or pass through a fine mesh sieve.

NOTE: For a refreshing flavor, add 1-inch (2.5 cm) cube of ginger root before blending.

Per 1 Cup (240 ml) Serving (unstrained): 124 Cal (39% from Fat, 32% from Protein, 29% from Carb); 11 g Protein; 6 g Tot Fat; 1 g Sat Fat; 10 g Carb; 4 g Fiber; 5 g Sugar; 5 mg Sodium; 0 mg Cholesterol

blending

RICE MILK

preparation: 10 minutes • processing: 1 minute • yield: 3 1/4 cups (780 ml)

2 cups (480 ml) water

1/2 cup (100 g) cooked brown rice, cooled

1/2-1 Tablespoon brown sugar or other sweetener, to taste

1. Place all ingredients into the Vitamix container in the order listed and secure lid.

2. Select Variable 1.

3. Turn machine on and slowly increase speed to Variable 10, then to High.

4. Blend for 1 minute or until desired consistency is reached.

NOTE: For a richer flavor, add 1/2 teaspoon vanilla extract before blending.

Per 1 Cup (240 ml) Serving: 42 Cal (5% from Fat, 7% from Protein, 88% from Carb); 1 g Protein; 0 g Tot Fat; 0 g Sat Fat; 9 g Carb; 1 g Fiber; 2 g Sugar; 3 mg Sodium; 0 mg Cholesterol

ALMOND MILK

preparation: 5 minutes • processing: 40 seconds • yield: 4 1/2 cups (1.0 l) unstrained or 2 3/4 cups (660 ml) strained

3 cups (720 ml) water

1 cup (140 g) raw almonds

sugar or sweetener, to taste (optional)

1. Place all ingredients into the Vitamix container in the order listed and secure lid.

2. Select Variable 1.

3. Turn machine on and slowly increase speed to Variable 10, then to High.

4. Blend for 40 seconds or until desired consistency is reached.

5. To obtain commercial-style almond milk, strain the milk through a nut milk bag or pass through a fine mesh sieve.

Per 1 Cup (240 ml) Serving (unstrained): 183 Cal (72% from Fat, 14% from Protein, 14% from Carb); 7 g Protein; 16 g Tot Fat; 1 g Sat Fat; 7 g Carb; 4 g Fiber; 1 g Sugar; 3 mg Sodium; 0 mg Cholesterol

SPINACH ARTICHOKE DIP

preparation: 30 minutes • processing: 20 seconds • bake time: 20-25 minutes
yield: 2 1/2 cups (600 g)

1/2 cup (120 g)
light mayonnaise

1/2 cup (120 g) light
sour cream

1/4-inch (.6 cm) slice
lemon, peeled

10 ounce (284 g)
package frozen chopped
spinach, thawed, drained

1/8 teaspoon salt

1/8 teaspoon black pepper

1 garlic clove, peeled

1/4 cup (25 g) grated
Parmesan cheese

1/2 cup (85 g) frozen and
cooked artichoke hearts
or canned artichoke
hearts, drained

1. Preheat oven to 350°F (180°C).

2. Place mayonnaise, sour cream, lemon, spinach, salt, pepper, garlic, and Parmesan cheese into the Vitamix container in the order listed and secure lid.

3. Select Variable 1.

4. Turn machine on and slowly increase speed to Variable 5.

5. Blend for 15 seconds, using the tamper to press the ingredients into the blades.

6. Add artichokes through the lid plug opening.

7. Blend for an additional 5 seconds.

8. Pour into a small oven-safe dish and bake uncovered for 20 to 25 minutes or until bubbly.

Per 2 Tablespoon (30 g) Serving: 63 Cal (81% from Fat, 9% from Protein, 10% from Carb); 1 g Protein; 6 g Tot Fat; 2 g Sat Fat; 2 g Carb; 1 g Fiber; 0 g Sugar; 84 mg Sodium; 6 mg Cholesterol

GUACAMOLE

preparation: 15 minutes • processing: 1 1/2 minutes • yield: 3 cups (720 g)

1 Roma tomato,
3 ounces (85 g),
quartered, divided use

4 ripe avocados, halved,
pitted, peeled, divided use

1/2 cup (40 g) chopped
red onion

2 Tablespoons (30 ml)
lemon juice

1/2 cup (8 g) fresh
cilantro leaves

1 teaspoon salt

1. Place 1/4 tomato, 1/2 an avocado, onion, lemon juice, cilantro, and salt into the Vitamix container in the order listed and secure lid.

2. Select Variable 2.

3. Turn machine on and blend for 20 seconds or until ingredients are mixed, using the tamper to push the ingredients into the blades while processing. Stop machine and remove lid.

4. Add remaining ingredients into the Vitamix container and secure lid.

5. Select Variable 2.

6. Turn machine on and blend for an additional 1 minute, using the tamper to press the ingredients into the blades.

7. Do not over mix. Leave chunky. Serve with tortilla chips.

NOTE: For a spicy guacamole, add 1/2 jalapeño pepper during Step 1.

Per 2 Tablespoon (30 g) Serving: 51 Cal (72% from Fat, 5% from Protein, 23% from Carb); 1 g Protein; 4 g Tot Fat; 1 g Sat Fat; 3 g Carb; 2 g Fiber; 0 g Sugar; 102 mg Sodium; 0 mg Cholesterol

blending

GAZPACHO

preparation: 15 minutes • processing: 20 seconds • yield: 4 1/4 cups (1.0 l)

1 1/2 cups (360 ml) fresh or canned tomato juice

1 1/2 Tablespoons red wine vinegar

2 Tablespoons (30 ml) olive oil

1 large ripe tomato, 11 ounces (312 g), quartered

1/2 cucumber, 7 1/2 ounces (213 g), peeled, quartered

1/2 small onion, 1 ounce (28 g), peeled

1/2 sweet green bell pepper, 4 ounces (114 g), seeded, halved

dash hot sauce

salt and pepper

1. Place tomato juice, vinegar, olive oil, tomato, cucumber, onion, and green pepper into the Vitamix container in the order listed and secure lid.

2. Select Variable 1.

3. Turn machine on and slowly increase speed to Variable 3.

4. Blend for 20 seconds, using the tamper to press the ingredients into the blades.

5. Season soup with hot sauce, salt, and pepper and serve immediately.

NOTE: Serve over chopped cucumbers and tomatoes.

Per 1 Cup (240 ml) Serving: 105 Cal (56% from Fat, 7% from Protein, 37% from Carb); 2 g Protein; 7 g Tot Fat; 1 g Sat Fat; 10 g Carb; 2 g Fiber; 7 g Sugar; 251 mg Sodium; 0 mg Cholesterol

BUTTER

preparation: 10 minutes • processing: 30 seconds • yield: 1 1/2 cups (360 g)

2 cups (480 ml) heavy whipping cream

1/8-1/4 teaspoon salt, to taste

1. Place cream into the Vitamix container and secure lid.

2. Select Variable 1.

3. Turn machine on and slowly increase speed to Variable 10, then to high.

4. Blend a few seconds until mixture is thick and stops circulating.

5. Reduce speed to Variable 5 and remove the lid plug.

6. Continue to process, using the tamper to press the butter into the blades, until mixture separates into liquid and solids, about 25 seconds.

7. Place butter in a fine strainer to drain off the liquid.

8. Remove butter to a bowl and add salt to taste. Work butter with a spatula to remove as much liquid as possible.

9. Store in an airtight container.

NOTE: Create flavored butters by adding sun-dried tomatoes, herbs, or cinnamon in Step 1.

Per 1 Tablespoon Serving: 34 Cal (95% from Fat, 2% from Protein, 3% from Carb); 0 g Protein; 4 g Tot Fat; 2 g Sat Fat; 0 g Carb; 0 g Fiber; 0 g Sugar; 28 mg Sodium; 14 mg Cholesterol

To make Whipped Cream: Omit salt, add 3 Tablespoons (38 g) sugar and 1 teaspoon vanilla extract in Step 1. Select Variable 1. Turn machine on and slowly increase speed to Variable 10, then to high. Blend for 3 to 5 seconds or until mixture stops circulating. Do not over mix. Serve within 2 hours.

CRANBERRY NUT BREAD

preparation: 15 minutes • processing: 30 seconds • bake time: 55-60 minutes
yield: 1 loaf (12 slices)

1 cup (100 g)
fresh cranberries

1 orange, peeled,
quartered

1-2-inch (2.5-5 cm)
strip of orange peel or
lemon peel

1/4 cup (60 ml) light
olive oil or vegetable oil

3/4 cup (180 ml) milk

1 cup (200 g) sugar

1 large egg

1 teaspoon vanilla extract

1 1/2 teaspoons
baking powder

1/2 teaspoon baking soda

1 teaspoon salt

2 cups (240 g) whole
wheat flour

1/2 cup (46 g)
chopped almonds

1. Preheat the oven to 350°F (180°C). Lightly coat an 8 1/2-inch x 4 1/2-inch (22 cm x 11 cm) loaf pan with vegetable cooking spray or shortening.

2. Place Vitamix container on base and secure lid. Select Variable 1. Turn machine on, remove the lid plug, and drop cranberries through lid plug opening just until chopped. Stop; scrape sides and remove chopped cranberries to a small bowl.

3. Place orange quarters, peel, oil, milk, sugar, egg, and vanilla into the Vitamix container in the order listed and secure lid.

4. Select Variable 1.

5. Turn machine on and slowly increase speed to Variable 10, then to High.

6. Blend for 30 seconds.

7. Combine baking powder, baking soda, salt, and whole wheat flour in a large-size mixing bowl; stir well.

8. Pour orange juice mixture into the dry ingredients, mixing by hand just until ingredients are moistened. Stir in chopped nuts and cranberries; do not over mix.

9. Spread the batter in the prepared loaf pan.

10. Bake for 55 to 60 minutes or until a toothpick inserted into the center comes out clean. Cool on wire rack 30 minutes, then carefully remove from loaf pan and allow to cool completely before slicing.

Per Slice: 235 Cal (33% from Fat, 8% from Protein, 59% from Carb); 5 g Protein; 9 g Tot Fat; 1 g Sat Fat; 36 g Carb; 4 g Fiber; 20 g Sugar; 320 mg Sodium; 19 mg Cholesterol

CARROT RAISIN MUFFINS

preparation: 15 minutes • processing: 30 seconds • bake time: 20-25 minutes
yield: 12 muffins

1 2/3 cups (200 g)
self-rising flour

1/2 teaspoon baking soda

1 teaspoon
ground cinnamon

1 teaspoon pumpkin
pie spice

3/4 cup (100 g) rough
chop carrots

2 large eggs

3/4 cup (150 g) sugar

2/3 cup (160 ml) light
olive oil

1 cup (165 g) raisins,
soaked in hot water
10 minutes, drained

1. Preheat the oven to 350°F (180°C). Spray a 12-cup muffin tin with cooking spray or line with paper liners.

2. Combine flour, baking soda, cinnamon, and pumpkin pie spice in a medium-size mixing bowl and stir lightly. Set aside.

3. Place carrots, eggs, sugar, and oil into the Vitamix container and secure lid.

4. Select Variable 1.

5. Turn machine on and slowly increase speed to Variable 5.

6. Blend for 30 seconds until thick and creamy.

7. Pour carrot mixture into flour mixture, mixing by hand to combine. Stir in raisins. Spoon the mixture into prepared muffin tin.

8. Bake for 20 to 25 minutes until golden brown. Cool on wire racks.

Per Muffin: 277 Cal (43% from Fat, 5% from Protein, 53% from Carb); 3 g Protein; 13 g Tot Fat;
2 g Sat Fat; 37 g Carb; 1 g Fiber; 21 g Sugar; 296 mg Sodium; 35 mg Cholesterol

APPLE PANCAKES

preparation: 15 minutes · processing: 15 seconds · yield: 10 pancakes

1 cup (120 g) whole wheat flour

1 Tablespoon baking powder

1/2 teaspoon baking soda

1/2 teaspoon salt

3 Tablespoons (38 g) sugar

1/4 teaspoon nutmeg

1 cup (240 ml) milk

1 large egg

1 1/2 teaspoons butter

1/4 teaspoon vanilla extract

1/2 medium apple, 3 ounces (85 g), seeded, cut into chunks

1. Combine flour, baking powder, baking soda, salt, sugar, and nutmeg in a medium-size mixing bowl and stir lightly. Set aside.

2. Place milk, egg, butter, vanilla extract, and apple into the Vitamix container in the order listed and secure lid.

3. Select Variable 1.

4. Turn machine on and slowly increase speed to Variable 8.

5. Blend for 15 seconds.

6. Pour wet mixture into dry mixture and mix by hand just until combined.

7. Let batter sit for 5 to 10 minutes before cooking to yield best texture and flavor.

Per Pancake: 88 Cal (21% from Fat, 14% from Protein, 65% from Carb); 3 g Protein; 2 g Tot Fat; 1 g Sat Fat; 15 g Carb; 2 g Fiber; 6 g Sugar; 346 mg Sodium; 28 mg Cholesterol

dry
CHOPPING

Here's another tedious chore that is so easy with the Vitamix® machine. Dry chopping is used for such things as carrots, onions, eggs, and cheese. With the Vitamix machine, these tasks are quick, easy, and require little cleanup. You decide how coarse or fine you want the finished product just by adjusting the Variable Speed Dial. The faster the speed, the finer the chop. Remember, the customized hammermill and cutting blades do all the work, so you don't have to. You can even combine some items used in the same recipe and save even more time.

DRY CHOPPING

dry
CHOPPING

dry chopping

MINCING ONIONS AND EGGS

1. Place the Vitamix container securely on the base, secure lid, and remove the lid plug.

2. Select Variable 3.

3. Turn machine on and drop hard boiled eggs or onion quarters onto the blades through the lid plug opening.

4. Continue processing until the desired texture is reached. Mince in small batches for best results.

CHOPPING CHEESE

4 ounces (114 g) firm cheese, such as cheddar, Monterey jack, or Swiss, cut into 1-inch (2.5 cm) cubes

1. Place Vitamix container on base and secure lid.

2. Select Variable 2.

3. Turn machine on and remove the lid plug.

4. Drop cheese cubes through the lid plug opening and process until desired consistency is reached. Remove cheese then process additional batches as needed.

NOTE: For best processing, process no more than 4 ounces (114 g) of firm cheese at a time.

CHOPPING CARROTS

5 ounces (142 g) carrots cut into 2-inch (5 cm) pieces

1. Place carrots into the Vitamix container and secure lid.

2. Select Variable 1.

3. Turn machine on and slowly increase speed to Variable 5.

4. Blend for 20 seconds.

NOTE: For best processing, process no more than 5 ounces (142 g) of carrots at a time.

dry chopping

GRATING HARD CHEESE

4 1/2 ounces (128 g) hard cheese, such as Parmesan, Romano, or Asiago, cut into 1-inch (2.5 cm) cubes

1. Place cheese into the Vitamix container and secure lid.

2. Select Variable 1.

3. Turn machine on and slowly increase speed to Variable 7.

4. Blend for 30 seconds.

NOTE: For best processing, process no more than 4 1/2 ounces (128 g) of hard cheese at a time.

MAKING FRESH BREAD CRUMBS

2 large slices soft, fresh bread, torn into 1-1 1/2-inch (2.5-4 cm) pieces

1. Place bread into the Vitamix container and secure lid.

2. Select Variable 1.

3. Turn machine on and slowly increase speed to Variable 8.

4. Blend for 10 to 15 seconds.

notes

wet CHOPPING

The difference between wet chopping and dry chopping is that this method uses water or another liquid as the medium that circulates the items being chopped. Wet chopping is recommended only for uncooked fruits or vegetables. Water draws the item into the blades resulting in a uniform chop. The type of chop, whether coarse or fine, is determined by the speed selected on the Variable Speed Dial. With wet chopping you can easily prepare vegetables for soups, salads, stir-frying, side dishes, and coleslaw. Wet chopping is also the recommended preparation for all raw vegetables where a uniform chop is required (e.g. salsa). However, when wet chopping ingredients for salsa, the moisture released by the vegetables allows the vegetables to circulate into the blades, so no additional liquid is needed. Plus there is no need to discard the liquid used in this process—save and use it in sauces and soups.

wet
CHOPPING

CHOPPING CABBAGE

1 head cabbage, cut into
1 1/2-inch (4 cm) wedges

1. Place wedges into the Vitamix container up to the 4 cup (960 ml) mark. Fill with water until cabbage floats off of blades and secure lid.

2. Select Variable 5.

3. Turn machine on and slowly increase speed to Variable 8. Stop machine.

4. Drain cabbage and remove to a bowl.

CRUSHING ICE

1. Fill the Vitamix container with ice cubes. Add water until ice floats off of blades and secure lid.

2. Select Variable 1.

3. Turn machine on and slowly increase speed to Variable 10. Stop machine.

4. Pour off water and use immediately.

SHREDDED POTATOES
FOR HASH BROWNS

5 Russet
potatoes, quartered

1. Place potatoes into the Vitamix container and fill to the 4 cup (960 ml) mark. Add water to the 6 cup (1.4 l) mark and secure lid.

2. Select Variable 5.

3. Turn machine on and blend for 10 seconds.

4. Drain well. Repeat with remaining potatoes. Press water out and use in your favorite hash brown recipe.

NOTE: This recipe may be reduced for smaller quantities.

wet chopping

CALIFORNIA SALSA

preparation: 10 minutes • processing: 30 seconds • yield: 2 cups (480 g)

1/2 medium onion,
2 1/2 ounces (70 g),
peeled, halved

1 jalapeño pepper,
1 1/2 ounces (43 g), seeds
and membranes removed

1/4 cup (4 g)
fresh cilantro leaves

1 teaspoon fresh
lemon juice

1/2 teaspoon salt

6 ripe Roma tomatoes,
quartered (24 quarters)

1. Place onion, jalapeño, cilantro, lemon juice, salt, and six of the tomato quarters into the Vitamix container in the order listed and secure lid.

2. Select Variable 1.

3. Turn machine on and slowly increase speed to Variable 5.

4. Blend for 20 seconds, using the tamper to press the ingredients into the blades.

5. Reduce speed to Variable 3 and remove the lid plug. Add the remaining tomato quarters through the lid plug opening. Continue to blend until desired consistency is reached, using the tamper to press the ingredients into the blades.

6. Do not over mix, leave chunky. Serve with tortilla chips.

NOTE: The size of Roma tomatoes varies greatly. Yield may vary from 2 to 4 cups.

Per 2 Tablespoon (30 g) Serving: 6 Cal (8% from Fat, 15% from Protein, 77% from Carb); 0 g Protein; 0 g Tot Fat; 0 g Sat Fat; 1 g Carb; 0 g Fiber; 1 g Sugar; 75 mg Sodium; 0 mg Cholesterol

PINEAPPLE SALSA

preparation: 20 minutes • processing: 15-20 seconds • yield: 2 1/2 cups (600 g)

2 Tablespoons (30 ml) olive oil

1/4 cup (40 g) chopped onion

1/2 cup (75 g) red bell pepper cut into 1-inch x 1-inch (2.5 x 2.5 cm) pieces

2 Tablespoons (2 g) fresh chopped cilantro leaves

1/2 lime, peeled

1/2 teaspoon salt

1/4 jalapeño pepper

3 cups (500 g) fresh pineapple, peeled, cut into large pieces

1. Place all ingredients into the Vitamix container in the order listed and secure lid.

2. Select Variable 1.

3. Turn machine on and slowly increase speed to Variable 3.

4. Blend for 15 to 20 seconds using the tamper to press the ingredients into the blades.

5. Do not over mix. Leave chunky. Serve with tortilla chips.

Per 2 Tablespoon (30 g) Serving: 28 Cal (42% from Fat, 4% from Protein, 55% from Carb); 0 g Protein; 1 g Tot Fat; 0 g Sat Fat; 4 g Carb; 1 g Fiber; 3 g Sugar; 60 mg Sodium; 0 mg Cholesterol

notes

making
FROZEN
treats

The most amazing dessert you'll make in your Vitamix machine is a
delicious frozen treat. And what's even more amazing is that you'll make
it in under a minute! The real secret is the high performance hammermill
and cutting blades that crush and cut up frozen ingredients in seconds.
The blade action produces a larger frozen surface area that releases coldness.
The Vitamix machine works so fast that it all happens in about 30 seconds,
so there's no time for the mixture to melt. It actually refreezes itself instantly
and creates a smooth and scrumptious soft-serve frozen treat.

making
FROZEN TREATS

RASPBERRY ZINGER

preparation: 10 minutes • processing: 30-60 seconds • yield: 3 1/2 cups (840 g)

1 cup (240 ml) milk

1/2 cup (100 g) sugar

1/2 teaspoon
vanilla extract

1 pound (454 g) frozen
unsweetened raspberries

1. Place all ingredients into the Vitamix container in the order listed and secure lid.

2. Select Variable 1.

3. Turn machine on and slowly increase speed to Variable 10, then to High. Use the tamper to press ingredients into the blades.

4. In about 30 to 60 seconds, the sound of the motor will change and four mounds should form.

5. Stop machine. Do not over mix or melting will occur. Serve immediately.

NOTE: For best results, allow frozen fruit to thaw at room temperature 5 minutes before blending.

Per 1/2 Cup (120 g) Serving: 138 Cal (10% from Fat, 6% from Protein, 85% from Carb); 2 g Protein; 2 g Tot Fat; 1 g Sat Fat; 31 g Carb; 4 g Fiber; 27 g Sugar; 14 mg Sodium; 3 mg Cholesterol

PEACH SOY SHERBET

preparation: 10 minutes • processing: 40-60 seconds • yield: 3 1/2 cups (840 g)

1 cup (240 ml) soy milk

1/4 cup (50 g) sugar

1/2 teaspoon
vanilla extract

1 pound (454 g) frozen
unsweetened peach slices

1. Place all ingredients into the Vitamix container in the order listed and secure lid.

2. Select Variable 1.

3. Turn machine on and slowly increase speed to Variable 10, then to High. Use the tamper to press ingredients into the blades.

4. In about 40 to 60 seconds, the sound of the motor will change and four mounds should form.

5. Stop machine. Do not over mix or melting will occur. Serve immediately.

NOTE: For best results, allow frozen fruit to thaw at room temperature 5 minutes before blending.

Per 1/2 Cup (120 g) Serving: 69 Cal (9% from Fat, 7% from Protein, 83% from Carb); 1 g Protein; 1 g Tot Fat; 0 g Sat Fat; 15 g Carb; 1 g Fiber; 12 g Sugar; 4 mg Sodium; 0 mg Cholesterol

MANGO YOGURT FREEZE

preparation: 10 minutes • processing: 40-60 seconds • yield: 3 cups (720 g)

1 cup (240 g)
vanilla yogurt

1 pound (454 g) frozen
mango chunks

1. Place all ingredients into the Vitamix container in the order listed and secure lid.

2. Select Variable 1.

3. Turn machine on and slowly increase speed to Variable 10, then to High. Use the tamper to press ingredients into the blades.

4. In about 40 to 60 seconds, the sound of the motor will change and four mounds should form in the mixture.

5. Stop machine. Do not over mix or melting will occur. Serve immediately.

NOTE: For best results, allow frozen fruit to thaw at room temperature 5 minutes before blending.

Per 1/2 Cup (120 g) Serving: 83 Cal (5% from Fat, 9% from Protein, 85% from Carb); 2 g Protein; 1 g Tot Fat; 0 g Sat Fat; 19 g Carb; 1 g Fiber; 17 g Sugar; 27 mg Sodium; 2 mg Cholesterol

CHOCOLATE AND COOKIES FREEZE

preparation: 10 minutes • processing: 30 seconds • yield: 5 cups (1.2 kg)

3 chocolate chip cookies

1 cup (240 ml) chocolate milk

1 Tablespoon honey

2 Tablespoons (10 g) cocoa powder

1/4 cup (60 g) chocolate chips

3 bananas, peeled, frozen

3 cups (720 ml) ice cubes

1. Place cookies into the Vitamix container and secure lid.

2. Select Variable 3.

3. Use On/Off switch to pulse 5 to 10 times to chop. Transfer to a bowl and set aside.

4. Put remaining ingredients into the Vitamix container in the order listed and secure lid.

5. Select Variable 1.

6. Turn machine on and slowly increase speed to Variable 10, then to High. Use the tamper to press ingredients into the blades.

7. In about 30 seconds, the sound of the motor will change and four mounds should form.

8. Stop machine. Stir in cookies and serve immediately.

NOTE: Hard and dry ice works best in this recipe.

Per 1/2 Cup (120 g) Serving: 115 Cal (26% from Fat, 5% from Protein, 69% from Carb); 2 g Protein; 4 g Tot Fat; 2 g Sat Fat; 21 g Carb; 2 g Fiber; 14 g Sugar; 27 mg Sodium; 3 mg Cholesterol

ORANGE SORBET

preparation: 10 minutes • processing: 30-40 seconds • yield: 3 1/2 cups (840 g)

2 medium oranges, peeled, halved

2 tablespoons (20 g) sugar

3 cups (720 ml) ice cubes

1. Place all ingredients into the Vitamix container in the order listed and secure lid.

2. Select Variable 1.

3. Turn machine on and slowly increase speed to Variable 10, then to High. Use the tamper to press ingredients into the blades.

4. In about 30 to 40 seconds, the sound of the motor will change and four mounds should form.

5. Stop machine. Do not over mix or melting will occur. Serve immediately.

NOTE: Hard and dry ice works best in this recipe.

Per 1/2 Cup (120 g) Serving: 34 Cal (1% from Fat, 4% from Protein, 95% from Carb); 0 g Protein; 0 g Tot Fat; 0 g Sat Fat; 9 g Carb; 1 g Fiber; 7 g Sugar; 0 mg Sodium; 0 mg Cholesterol

STRAWBERRY LIME SORBET

preparation: 10 minutes • processing: 30 seconds • yield: 3 1/2 cups (840 g)

1 cup (240 ml) water

1/4 cup (50 g) sugar

1/2 lime, peeled

1 pound (454 g) frozen unsweetened strawberries

1. Place all ingredients into the Vitamix container in the order listed and secure lid.

2. Select Variable 1.

3. Turn machine on and slowly increase speed to Variable 10, then to High. Use the tamper to press ingredients into the blades.

4. In about 30 seconds, the sound of the motor will change and four mounds should form.

5. Stop machine. Do not over mix or melting will occur. Serve immediately.

NOTE: For best results, allow frozen fruit to thaw at room temperature 5 minutes before blending.

Per 1/2 Cup (120 g) Serving: 52 Cal (1% from Fat, 2% from Protein, 97% from Carb); 0 g Protein; 0 g Tot Fat; 0 g Sat Fat; 14 g Carb; 1 g Fiber; 10 g Sugar; 2 mg Sodium; 0 mg Cholesterol

notes

HEATING

It's simple science—and simply amazing with Vitamix®!
Heating with the Vitamix machine starts with fresh, whole
produce and in four to six minutes you'll get a fresh,
hot soup complete with all the nutrients. The Vitamix blades
turn so fast they generate enough friction to create cooking heat.
Simply toss in the ingredients identified in the recipe, blend
for the appropriate time and you'll experience delicious,
whole vegetable soups and sauces with no peeling
or seeding required.

⚠CAUTION		
	Never Start on Speeds Above 1 with Hot Liquids to Avoid Possible Burns. Use Caution; escaping steam or splashes may scald. Lock the lid. This will prevent expansion from affecting the position of the lid when the machine is turned on. Start on Variable 1, slowly increase to 10.	

HEATING

HEATING

CHOCOLATE ORANGE FONDUE

preparation: 15 minutes • processing: 4-5 minutes • yield: 2 cups (480 ml)

1 cup (240 ml) heavy whipping cream

2 teaspoons grated orange peel

8 ounces (227 g) semi-sweet baking chocolate, rough chopped

3 Tablespoons (45 ml) Grand Marnier

1. Place cream, orange peel, and chocolate into the Vitamix container in the order listed and secure lid.

2. Select Variable 1.

3. Turn machine on and slowly increase speed to Variable 10, then to High.

4. Blend for 4 to 5 minutes using the tamper to press the ingredients into the blades. Mixture will be smooth and warm.

5. Pour mixture into fondue pot.

6. Stir in Grand Marnier.

Per 2 Tablespoon (30 g) Serving: 111 Cal (56% from Fat, 3% from Protein, 42% from Carb); 1 g Protein; 6 g Tot Fat; 4 g Sat Fat; 11 g Carb; 1 g Fiber; 9 g Sugar; 3 mg Sodium; 11 mg Cholesterol

Dippers may include sponge cake, pound cake, sliced apples, sliced pears, marshmallows, strawberries, bananas, and fresh pineapple chunks.

TRADITIONAL CHEESE FONDUE

preparation: 15 minutes * processing: 5 minutes * yield: 4 cups (960 ml)

3/4 cup (180 ml) dry
white wine

3/4 cup (180 ml) water

1 1/2 Tablespoons Kirsch
(optional)

2 Tablespoons (16 g)
cornstarch

1/4 teaspoon nutmeg

1 teaspoon ground
black pepper

8 ounces (227 g) cubed
Gruyère cheese

8 ounces (227 g) cubed
Emmental cheese

1. Place all ingredients into the Vitamix container in the
    order listed and secure lid.

2. Select Variable 1.

3. Turn machine on and slowly increase speed to
    Variable 10, then to High.

4. Blend for 5 minutes until mixture is smooth and warm.

5. Pour mixture into fondue pot.

Per 2 Tablespoon (30 g) Serving: 62 Cal (66% from Fat, 28% from Protein, 7% from Carb); 4 g Protein;
4 g Tot Fat; 3 g Sat Fat; 1 g Carb; 0 g Fiber; 0 g Sugar; 38 mg Sodium; 14 mg Cholesterol

Cheese fondues should be used immediately since they rarely
remain smooth when reheated. Leftover cheese fondue can make
an excellent base for a soup or pasta sauce.

Dippers may include cubed country French bread, mushroom caps,
steamed or grilled asparagus spears, steamed or grilled broccoli,
and cauliflower.

BROCCOLI CHEESE SOUP

preparation: 10 minutes • processing: 5-6 minutes • yield: 2 cups (480 ml)

1 cup (240 ml) milk

1/2 cup (60 g) shredded cheddar cheese

1 1/2 cups (150 g) fresh or frozen broccoli or cauliflower florets, steamed

1 teaspoon diced onion

1 chicken or vegetable bouillon cube

1. Place all ingredients into the Vitamix container in the order listed and secure lid.

2. Select Variable 1.

3. Turn machine on and slowly increase speed to Variable 10, then to High.

4. Blend for 5 to 6 minutes or until heavy steam escapes from the vented lid.

NOTE: A healthy way to thicken this soup is to add a 1/4 cup (65 g) canned and drained cannellini beans in Step 1.

Per 1 Cup (240 ml) Serving: 135 Cal (24% from Fat, 41% from Protein, 34% from Carb); 14 g Protein; 4 g Tot Fat; 2 g Sat Fat; 12 g Carb; 2 g Fiber; 2 g Sugar; 304 mg Sodium; 12 mg Cholesterol

Steam and reserve an extra cup of broccoli or cauliflower florets to add to your finished soup when serving.

TOMATO ALFREDO SAUCE

preparation: 10 minutes • processing: 6 minutes • yield: 3 1/4 cups (780 ml)

3 Roma tomatoes,
9 ounces (256 g), halved

1/2 cup (120 ml) milk

4 ounces (114 g)
cream cheese

1 Tablespoon butter

1 1/2 Tablespoons
all-purpose flour

salt and pepper

1. Place tomatoes, milk, cream cheese, butter, and flour into the Vitamix container in the order listed and secure lid.

2. Select Variable 1.

3. Turn machine on and slowly increase speed to Variable 10, then to High.

4. Blend for 6 minutes or until heavy steam escapes from the vented lid.

5. Season to taste with salt and pepper.

Per 1/4 Cup (60 ml) Serving: 50 Cal (75% from Fat, 9% from Protein, 15% from Carb); 1 g Protein;
4 g Tot Fat; 3 g Sat Fat; 2 g Carb; 0 g Fiber; 1 g Sugar; 31 mg Sodium; 13 mg Cholesterol

ACORN SQUASH SOUP

preparation: 30 minutes • processing: 5-6 minutes • yield: 4 1/2 cups (1.0 l)

2 cups (480 ml) chicken broth

1/2 cup (120 ml) evaporated milk

1/2 medium acorn squash, 1 pound (454 g), roasted, peeled, seeded, cooled

1 teaspoon maple syrup

pinch of nutmeg

1/4 teaspoon cinnamon

salt and pepper to taste

1. Heat chicken broth and evaporated milk over medium heat in a saucepan, about 4 minutes.

2. Place all ingredients into the Vitamix container in the order listed and secure lid.

3. Select Variable 1.

4. Turn machine on and slowly increase speed to Variable 10, then to High.

5. Blend for 5 to 6 minutes or until heavy steam escapes from the vented lid.

Per 1 Cup (240 ml) Serving: 110 Cal (22% from Fat, 17% from Protein, 61% from Carb); 5 g Protein; 3 g Tot Fat; 2 g Sat Fat; 18 g Carb; 4 g Fiber; 1 g Sugar; 65 mg Sodium; 8 mg Cholesterol

To roast squash easily, split in half, scoop out the seeds and place flesh side down on a lightly greased baking pan. Pierce skin and bake 350°F (180°C) for 30 minutes. Or place in microwave-safe baking dish flesh side down, cover and microwave on High for 10 minutes or until fork tender.

Blend times are for room temperature ingredients. If using freshly cooked ingredients, blend times may be reduced.

CREAM OF ASPARAGUS SOUP

preparation: 15 minutes • processing: 5-6 minutes • yield: 5 cups (1.2 l)

1 1/2 cups (360 ml) chicken broth

1 1/2 pounds (680 g) asparagus spears, cooked, cooled, cut into thirds, reserve 1 cup (134 g) chopped

1/2 cup (120 ml) heavy cream

salt and pepper

1. Place chicken broth and asparagus into the Vitamix container and secure lid.

2. Select Variable 1.

3. Turn machine on and slowly increase speed to Variable 10, then to High.

4. Blend for 5 to 6 minutes or until smooth.

5. Reduce speed to Variable 5 and remove the lid plug. Pour in heavy cream through the lid plug opening.

6. Blend for an additional 30 seconds. Serve immediately over reserved asparagus pieces. Season to taste with salt and pepper.

NOTE: Steam asparagus for about 10 minutes or until tender. Let cool 10 minutes before blending.

Per 1 Cup (240 ml) Serving: 80 Cal (52% from Fat, 22% from Protein, 27% from Carb); 5 g Protein; 5 g Tot Fat; 3 g Sat Fat; 6 g Carb; 3 g Fiber; 3 g Sugar; 236 mg Sodium; 16 mg Cholesterol

GINGERED CARROT ORANGE SOUP

preparation: 20 minutes • processing: 4-5 minutes • cook time: 15-20 minutes
yield: 3 3/4 cups (900 ml)

1/2 pound (227 g) carrots, chopped

1 medium onion, 4 ounces (114 g), peeled, sliced

1/2-inch (1.3 cm) cube of fresh peeled ginger

1 Tablespoon butter

2 cups (480 ml) chicken or vegetable broth, divided use

1 1/2 oranges, peeled, halved

1/2-inch (1.3 cm) square piece orange peel

salt and pepper

1. Sauté carrots, onions, and ginger in butter over medium heat until soft, about 10 to 15 minutes.

2. Add 1 cup (240 ml) broth and cook an additional 3 minutes.

3. Place oranges, orange peel, cooked vegetable mixture, and remaining broth into the Vitamix container and secure lid.

4. Select Variable 1.

5. Turn machine on and slowly increase speed to Variable 10, then to High.

6. Blend for 4 to 5 minutes or until heavy steam escapes from the vented lid.

7. Season to taste with salt and pepper. Serve immediately.

⚠ **CAUTION**

Contents Will Be Hot.

NOTE: Garnish with light sour cream and chopped cilantro.

Per 1 Cup (240 ml) Serving: 126 Cal (28% from Fat, 13% from Protein, 59% from Carb); 4 g Protein; 4 g Tot Fat; 2 g Sat Fat; 19 g Carb; 4 g Fiber; 11 g Sugar; 457 mg Sodium; 8 mg Cholesterol

TORTILLA SOUP

preparation: 15 minutes • processing: 5-6 minutes • yield: 2 1/4 cups (540 ml) without optional ingredients

SOUP BASE

1 1/2 cups (360 ml) chicken, beef, or vegetable broth

1/2 large Roma tomato, 1 1/2 ounces (43 g)

1/2 medium carrot, 1 ounce (28 g)

1/2 large stalk celery, 1 ounce (28 g)

2 Tablespoons (20 g) chopped onion

1 garlic clove, peeled

1 Tablespoon chopped yellow squash (1 thin slice)

2 Tablespoons (20 g) chopped red bell pepper (1 thin slice)

1 cup (90 g) sliced cabbage

1 white mushroom

salt and pepper to taste

1 teaspoon taco seasoning

dash cumin

OPTIONAL INGREDIENTS

1/4 cup (35 g) cooked chicken, chunked

1/4 fresh jalapeño

2 Tablespoons (15 g) sliced olives

2 Tablespoons (25 g) unsalted canned corn, drained

1 ounce (30 g) tortilla chips

1/4 cup (33 g) cheddar cheese

1. Place all soup base ingredients into the Vitamix container in the order listed and secure lid.

2. Select Variable 1.

3. Turn machine on and slowly increase speed to Variable 10, then to High.

4. Blend for 5 to 6 minutes or until heavy steam escapes from the vented lid.

5. If adding optional ingredients, reduce speed to Variable 3 and remove the lid plug.

6. Drop ingredients through the lid plug opening.

7. Blend for an additional 10 seconds.

Per 1 Cup (240 ml) Serving (without optional ingredients): 56 Cal (18% from Fat, 33% from Protein, 50% from Carb); 5 g Protein; 1 g Tot Fat; 0 g Sat Fat; 7 g Carb; 2 g Fiber; 4 g Sugar; 546 mg Sodium; 0 mg Cholesterol

CHICKEN POTATO SPINACH SOUP

preparation: 15 minutes • processing: 5-6 minutes (See step 4.) • yield: 4 1/2 cups (1.0 l)

1 cup (240 ml)
chicken broth

1 1/2 cups (360 ml) milk

1/4 cup (40 g)
chopped onion

3 medium
Russet potatoes,
14 1/2 ounces (412 g),
baked, halved, cooled,
divided use

1/8 teaspoon
dried rosemary

1 Tablespoon spinach,
cooked or frozen, thawed

5 ounces (140 g) skinless,
boneless chicken breast,
cooked and diced

1/2 teaspoon kosher salt

1/2 teaspoon black pepper

1. Place broth, milk, onion, two potatoes, and rosemary into the Vitamix container in the order listed and secure lid.

2. Select Variable 1.

3. Turn machine on and slowly increase speed to Variable 10, then to High.

4. Blend for 5 to 6 minutes or until heavy steam escapes from the vented lid.

5. Reduce speed to Variable 3 and remove the lid plug.

6. Add spinach, one potato, and chicken through the lid plug opening.

7. Blend an additional 5 to 10 seconds.

NOTE: Blend times are for room temperature ingredients. If using freshly cooked ingredients, blend times may be reduced.

Per 1 Cup (240 ml) Serving: 201 Cal (20% from Fat, 33% from Protein, 47% from Carb); 17 g Protein; 4 g Tot Fat; 2 g Sat Fat; 23 g Carb; 2 g Fiber; 5 g Sugar; 535 mg Sodium; 35 mg Cholesterol

notes

grinding in the
WET BLADE
container

Our wet blade container is best suited for grinding foods that contain moisture. The wet blades draw the mixture down and into the blender for proper processing and the customized hammermill and cutting blades do all the work for you. Nut-butters are best done with the wet blades and can be used in many delicious recipes.

grinding in the wet
BLADE CONTAINER

PEANUT BUTTER

preparation: 5 minutes • processing: 1-2 minutes • yield: 1 3/4 cups (420 g)

3 cups (440 g) unsalted roasted peanuts

NOTICE: Over-processing will cause serious overheating to your machine and can cause damage to your container. Do not process for more than 1 minute after mixture starts circulating.

1. Place nuts into the Vitamix container and secure lid.

2. Select Variable 1.

3. Turn machine on and slowly increase speed to Variable 10, then to High.

4. Use the tamper to press the ingredients into the blades.

5. In 1 minute you will hear a high-pitched chugging sound. Keep using the tamper until the peanut butter begins to flow freely through the blades, the motor sound will change and become low and laboring. Stop machine.

6. Store in an airtight container in refrigerator. It can also be frozen for longer storage.

Per 2 Tablespoon (30 g) Serving: 183 Cal (71% from Fat, 15% from Protein, 14% from Carb); 7 g Protein; 16 g Tot Fat; 2 g Sat Fat; 7 g Carb; 3 g Fiber; 1 g Sugar; 2 mg Sodium; 0 mg Cholesterol

Mix and match different varieties of nuts to make your own signature blend. Do not process more than 3 cups (440 g) at a time.

notes

grinding in the
DRY BLADE
container

A dry blade container, specifically designed for grinding grains and rice, may be purchased separately. While the wet blade container is able to accomplish these tasks, the dry blade container will complete these processes more efficiently and is therefore recommended. The container with the blades marked "D" for dry is used to grind whole grains into flours and takes only one minute in your new Vitamix® machine. Take whole wheat berries and turn them into wonderful fresh breads, rolls, and hot cereals. Even beans, rice, and tapioca are easily ground into flours for use in gluten free recipes. Grinding your own grains will give you all the nutritional benefits of preservative-free, homemade bread.

grinding in the dry
BLADE CONTAINER

POWDERED SUGAR

preparation: 10 minutes • processing: 40 seconds • yield: 1 1/2 cups (180 g)

1 1/2 cups (300 g)
granulated sugar

1 Tablespoon cornstarch

1. Place sugar into the Vitamix container and secure lid.

2. Select Variable 1.

3. Turn machine on and slowly increase speed to Variable 10, then to High.

4. Blend for 30 seconds. Stop machine.

5. Remove the lid plug. Add cornstarch through the lid plug opening. Replace lid plug.

6. Select Variable 1.

7. Turn machine on and slowly increase speed to Variable 10, then to High.

8. Blend an additional 10 seconds.

9. Let powder settle before removing the lid.

Per 1 Teaspoon Serving: 17 Cal (0% from Fat, 0% from Protein, 100% from Carb); 0 g Protein;
0 g Tot Fat; 0 g Sat Fat; 4 g Carb; 0 g Fiber; 4 g Sugar; 0 mg Sodium; 0 mg Cholesterol

Adding cornstarch to powdered sugar prevents the sugar from caking and improves flow. If using immediately, cornstarch is optional.

WHOLE GRAIN FLOUR

preparation: 5 minutes • processing: 1 minute • yield: up to 3 1/4 cups (390 g)

1/4-2 cups (50-400 g) whole kernel grain

1. Place up to 2 cups (400 g) whole kernel grain into the Vitamix container and secure lid.

2. Select Variable 1.

3. Turn machine on and slowly increase speed to Variable 10, then to High.

4. Grind to desired degree of fineness (refer to the chart for recommended grinding times). The longer the machine runs, the finer the consistency of the flour, up to 1 minute.

Whole Kernel Wheat Measurement	Grinding Time	Speed	Approximate Flour Yield	Degree of Fineness
3/4 cup (144 g)	1 minute	VAR - HIGH	1 cup (120 g) + 2 1/2 teaspoons	very fine
1 cup (192 g)	1 minute	VAR - HIGH	1 1/2 cups (180 g)	very fine
1 1/4 cups (240 g)	1 minute	VAR - HIGH	1 3/4 cups (210 g) + 2 Tablespoons (15 g)	very fine
1 1/2 cups (288 g)	1 minute	VAR - HIGH	2 1/3 cups (280 g) + 1 Tablespoon (8 g)	very fine
1 3/4 cups (336 g)	1 minute	VAR - HIGH	2 1/2 cups (300 g) + 3 Tablespoons (22 g)	very fine
2 cups (384 g)	1 minute	VAR - HIGH	3 1/4 cups (390 g)	very fine

At room temperature, flour will stay fresh for a month. In the refrigerator, two months. For longer storage, flour can be frozen 6 months to a year. Bring to room temperature the amount you will need for baking.

MAKING DRY BREAD CRUMBS

2 slices wheat or white bread, dried or toasted, broken into pieces

1. Place bread into the Vitamix dry blade container and secure lid.

2. Select Variable 1.

3. Turn machine on and slowly increase speed to Variable 8.

4. Blend for 30 seconds.

notes

KNEADING

Start with fresh whole grains packed with nutrients and turn them into healthy homemade bread in one smooth operation. Yes, the Vitamix® machine grinds the grain and even kneads the dough so you will never need to touch it. Most recipes can be made in the dry blade container with little effort. Making bread from start to finish is so quick and easy, you can make healthy, preservative-free bread fresh daily. Bread made the Vitamix way is superior to commercially produced white bread in many different ways...more dietary fiber, more vitamins and fabulous, fresh, home-baked taste!

KNEADING

KNEADING

WHOLE WHEAT BREAD

preparation: 10 minutes • processing: 35 seconds • bake time: 35 minutes
yield: 1 loaf (12 slices)

1 package (1 Tablespoon)
active dry yeast

1 1/4 cups (300 ml) warm water,
105°F-115°F (40°C-46°C)

1 Tablespoon honey

1 1/2 cups (270 g) whole kernel wheat or
2 1/4 cups (270 g) whole wheat flour

1 teaspoon salt

1 Tablespoon light olive or grapeseed oil

1 teaspoon lemon juice

1 egg white mixed with 1 Tablespoon
water, optional (for brushing dough
before baking)

1. To proof the yeast, combine warm water, honey, and yeast.
   Stir quickly to combine. Set aside for 5 minutes.

2. **When starting with whole kernel wheat:** Place wheat and
   salt into the Vitamix DRY BLADE container and secure
   lid. Select Variable 1. Turn machine on and slowly increase
   speed to Variable 10, then to High. Grind wheat for 1 minute.
   (Do not over process.) Stop the machine to allow the flour
   to cool for a few minutes.

   When starting with whole wheat flour: Place flour and
   salt into the Vitamix DRY BLADE container and secure lid.
   Select Variable 1. Turn machine on and slowly increase
   speed to Variable 6. Blend until a hole forms in the center
   of the mixture, about 5 seconds.

3. Select Variable 3. Turn machine on and remove the lid plug.
   Pour oil, lemon juice, and yeast mixture through the lid plug
   opening. Stop machine and replace lid plug.

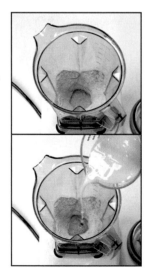

4. Select High speed. Quickly turn machine On and Off two times. Stop machine and remove lid.

5. While the dough rests, lightly coat an 8 1/2-inch x 4 1/2-inch (22 cm x 11 cm) loaf pan with vegetable cooking spray or shortening.

6. Use a nylon spatula to scrape the sides of the Vitamix container. Pull the dough away from the container sides and into the center of the mixture. Replace lid.

7. Select High speed. Quickly turn the machine On and Off five times. Add additional water, 1 Tablespoon at a time, only if dough seems exceptionally dry. Repeat process five times, scraping the sides of the container until the dough binds together into a soft, elastic mixture.

8. To remove the dough from the container, turn the machine on and off five times (to assist in lifting the dough up and away from the blades). Invert the container over the prepared pan and let the dough fall into the pan. Use a wet nylon spatula to remove any remaining dough.

9. Use a wet or oiled nylon spatula (or lightly floured fingers) to shape the loaf. Allow the dough to rise, covered with a clean, dry kitchen towel, until the top of it reaches the top of the bread pan, about 20 to 25 minutes.

10. If desired, brush the loaf quickly and gently with the egg white wash and make three to four diagonal slits about 1/4-inch (.6 cm) deep on the top of the loaf using a sharp, serrated knife.

11. Bake in a heated 350°F (180°C) for 35 minutes or until bread is well browned and reaches an internal temperature of 190°F (88°C) when tested with an instant read thermometer.

12. Cool on wire rack 10 minutes, then carefully remove from the pan and allow to cool completely before slicing.

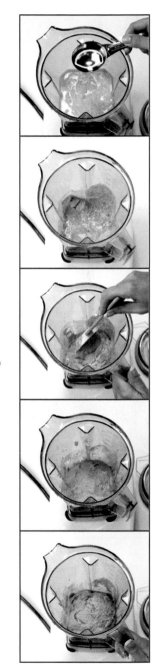

notes

EMULSIFY

The power of the Vitamix® lets you easily combine ingredients into emulsions, such as mayonnaise, aioli, and salad dressings. An added benefit of the Vitamix machine is the ability to add whole ingredients like fruits and vegetables to your emulsions, unlocking fresh flavors and healthy nutrients. Once you try homemade emulsions in your Vitamix, you'll never buy store bought again!

NOTICE: Do not process for longer than one minute after all ingredients have been added. Over-processing recipes made with large amounts of oil may cause overheating to occur and cause the recipe to fail and damage your container.

EMULSIFY

emulsify

BASIC VINAIGRETTE

preparation: 10 minutes • processing: 30-35 seconds • yield: 1 1/4 cups (300 ml)

3/4 cup (180 ml) olive oil

1/4 cup (60 ml) red or white vinegar

1 teaspoon Dijon mustard

1/4 teaspoon black pepper

1/2 teaspoon salt

1/4 cup (15 g) favorite fresh herbs

1. Place all ingredients into the Vitamix container in the order listed and secure lid.

2. Select Variable 1.

3. Turn machine on and slowly increase speed to Variable 10, then to High.

4. Blend for 30 to 35 seconds.

Per 2 Tablespoon (30 ml) Serving: 145 Cal (99% from Fat, 0% from Protein, 1% from Carb); 0 g Protein; 16 g Tot Fat; 2 g Sat Fat; 0 g Carb; 0 g Fiber; 0 g Sugar; 124 mg Sodium; 0 mg Cholesterol

RASPBERRY VINAIGRETTE

preparation: 10 minutes • processing: 20 seconds • yield: 1 3/4 cups (420 ml)

3/4 cup (180 ml) olive oil

1/4 cup (60 ml) apple cider or raspberry vinegar

1/4 cup (60 ml) water

1 teaspoon salt

2 Tablespoons (30 ml) honey

1 teaspoon dried basil

1/2 cup (60 g) fresh or frozen red raspberries

1. Place all ingredients into the Vitamix container in the order listed and secure lid.

2. Select Variable 1.

3. Turn machine on and slowly increase speed to Variable 10, then to High.

4. Blend for 20 seconds.

Per 2 Tablespoon (30 ml) Serving: 121 Cal (83% from Fat, 0% from Protein, 16% from Carb); 0 g Protein; 12 g Tot Fat; 2 g Sat Fat; 5 g Carb; 0 g Fiber; 5 g Sugar; 169 mg Sodium; 0 mg Cholesterol

BALSAMIC CITRUS DRESSING

preparation: 15 minutes • processing: 45 seconds • yield: 2 cups (480 ml)

1/4 cup (60 ml)
balsamic vinegar

2 Tablespoons (30 ml)
lime juice or
1/2 lime, peeled

3 medium oranges,
peeled, halved

4 green onions,
white part only, or
1/4 cup (25 g) chopped

2 small garlic
cloves, peeled

2 Tablespoons (25 g)
sugar or other sweetener
of choice

1/8 teaspoon white pepper

1 teaspoon salt

1/2 cup (120 ml) olive oil

1. Place vinegar, lime juice, oranges, green onions, garlic, sugar, pepper, and salt into the Vitamix container in the order listed and secure lid.

2. Select Variable 1.

3. Turn machine on and slowly increase speed to Variable 10, then to High.

4. Blend for 30 seconds or until smooth.

5. Reduce speed to Variable 3 and remove lid plug.

6. Pour oil in a thin stream through the lid plug opening until thoroughly emulsified.

7. Refrigerate in airtight container. Bring to room temperature and shake before serving over salad.

Per 2 Tablespoon (30 ml) Serving: 81 Cal (72% from Fat, 1% from Protein, 27% from Carb); 0 g Protein; 7 g Tot Fat; 1 g Sat Fat; 6 g Carb; 1 g Fiber; 4 g Sugar; 148 mg Sodium; 0 mg Cholesterol

PESTO SAUCE

preparation: 10 minutes • processing: 30 seconds • yield: 3/4 cup (180 ml)

1/2 cup (120 ml) olive oil

1/2 cup (50 g) grated Parmesan cheese

3 garlic cloves, peeled

2 cups (48 g) fresh basil leaves

3 Tablespoons (25 g) pine nuts

salt and pepper

1. Place olive oil, Parmesan cheese, garlic, basil, and pine nuts into the Vitamix container in the order listed and secure lid.

2. Select Variable 1.

3. Turn machine on and slowly increase speed to Variable 7.

4. Blend for 30 seconds, using the tamper to press the ingredients into the blades.

5. Season to taste with salt and pepper.

NOTE: Recipe yields enough sauce to coat 1 pound (454 g) of pasta.

Per 2 Tablespoon (30 g) Serving: 229 Cal (89% from Fat, 7% from Protein, 3% from Carb); 4 g Protein; 23 g Tot Fat; 4 g Sat Fat; 2 g Carb; 1 g Fiber; 0 g Sugar; 129 mg Sodium; 7 mg Cholesterol

emulsify

MAYONNAISE

preparation: 10 minutes • processing: 1 minute • yield: 2 1/2 cups (600 g)

3 large pasteurized eggs

1 1/4 teaspoons
dry mustard

1/2-1 teaspoon salt

1/4 cup (60 ml)
lemon juice

1 1/2 cups (360 ml)
canola oil

1. Place eggs, dry mustard, salt, and lemon juice into the Vitamix container in the order listed and secure lid.

2. Select Variable 1.

3. Turn machine on and slowly increase speed to Variable 10, then to High. Remove the lid plug.

4. While machine is running, slowly pour oil through the lid plug opening into the container. As mixture begins to thicken, the oil may be added at a faster rate. Process should take no longer than 60 seconds.

5. Stop machine and stir in any oil sitting on top.

6. Refrigerate in a separate container and use within 2 to 4 weeks.

NOTE: To make Aioli, add 3 peeled garlic cloves in Step 1 and substitute light olive oil for the canola oil. Proceed with rest of recipe.

Per 1 Tablespoon Serving: 79 Cal (97% from Fat, 3% from Protein, 1% from Carb); 1 g Protein; 9 g Tot Fat; 1 g Sat Fat; 0 g Carb; 0 g Fiber; 0 g Sugar; 36 mg Sodium; 18 mg Cholesterol

CAESAR SALAD DRESSING

preparation: 15 minutes • processing: 20 seconds • yield: 1 cup (240 ml)

1/2 cup (120 ml) olive oil

2 large pasteurized egg yolks

1 garlic clove, peeled

3 Tablespoons (45 ml) lemon juice

1/3 cup (33 g) grated Parmesan cheese

1 Tablespoon anchovy paste or anchovy filets

1/2 teaspoon salt

1/8 teaspoon dry mustard

black pepper to taste

1. Place all ingredients into the Vitamix container in the order listed and secure lid.

2. Select Variable 1.

3. Turn machine on and slowly increase speed to Variable 10, then to High.

4. Blend for 20 seconds.

Per 2 Tablespoon (30 ml) Serving: 154 Cal (92% from Fat, 6% from Protein, 2% from Carb); 2 g Protein; 16 g Tot Fat; 3 g Sat Fat; 1 g Carb; 0 g Fiber; 0 g Sugar; 233 mg Sodium; 55 mg Cholesterol

PURÉE

One of the many highlights of the Vitamix machine is the ability to create smooth, silky purées in seconds. You can easily process fruits, vegetables and other ingredients for dips, spreads, syrups and soups, creating delicious preservative-free meals. The power of the Vitamix machine saves you time in this process, too—all you have to do is place your ingredients into the container and blend until you have the perfect purée.

PURÉE

PURÉE

purée

FRESH BLUEBERRY SYRUP

preparation: 10 minutes • processing: 2-3 minutes • yield: 2 cups (480 ml)

1 teaspoon lemon juice

3/4 cup (100 g) sugar

3 cups (454 g) fresh or frozen, thawed blueberries

1. Place all ingredients into the Vitamix container in the order listed and secure lid.

2. Select Variable 1.

3. Turn machine on and slowly increase speed to Variable 10, then to High.

4. Blend for 2 to 3 minutes, using the tamper to press the ingredients into the blades.

5. For a thicker, more traditional syrup place mixture in a pot and cook on medium heat for 30 minutes. Use on pancakes, waffles or crêpes.

NOTE: Mix 1 ounce (30 ml) of syrup with 8-12 ounces (240-360 ml) of club soda and ice for a refreshing beverage.

Per 1/4 Cup (60 ml) Serving: 104 Cal (1% from Fat, 1% from Protein, 97% from Carb); 0 g Protein; 0 g Tot Fat; 0 g Sat Fat; 27 g Carb; 1 g Fiber; 24 g Sugar; 1 mg Sodium; 0 mg Cholesterol

Any fresh fruit or frozen, thawed fruit can be substituted in place of blueberries. Adjust sugar down or up depending on natural sweetness and ripeness of fruit.

purée

HUMMUS

preparation: 10 minutes • processing: 45 seconds • yield: 3 1/2 cups (840 g)

1 Tablespoon olive oil

1/4 cup (60 ml) lemon juice

1/4 cup (35 g) raw sesame seeds

15-ounce (425 g) can chickpeas (garbanzos), with liquid

15-ounce (425 g) can chickpeas (garbanzos), drained

1 garlic clove, peeled

1 teaspoon cumin

salt to taste

1. Place olive oil, lemon juice, sesame seeds, can of chickpeas with liquid, can of drained chickpeas, garlic, and cumin into the Vitamix container in the order listed and secure lid.

2. Select Variable 1.

3. Turn machine on and slowly increase speed to Variable 10, then to High.

4. Blend for 45 seconds, using the tamper to press the ingredients into the blades.

5. Season to taste with salt.

NOTE: If using bulk canned garbanzo beans or cooked dried beans, use 20 ounces (568 g) beans and 5 ounces (75 ml) liquid or water.

Per 2 Tablespoon (30 g) Serving: 53 Cal (25% from Fat, 14% from Protein, 60% from Carb); 2 g Protein; 2 g Tot Fat; 0 g Sat Fat; 8 g Carb; 2 g Fiber; 0 g Sugar; 103 mg Sodium; 0 mg Cholesterol

FRESH TOMATO SAUCE

preparation: 15 minutes • processing: 1 minute • cook time: 20-30 minutes
yield: 2 cups (480 ml)

1/2 teaspoon fresh
lemon juice

6 medium Roma
tomatoes, 18 ounces
(511 g), quartered

1 small onion, 2 ounces
(56 g), peeled, halved

1 small carrot, 1 1/2 ounces
(43 g), halved

2 Tablespoons (30 ml)
tomato paste

1 garlic clove, peeled

1/2 teaspoon dried basil

1/2 teaspoon
dried oregano

1/2 teaspoon brown sugar

1/4 teaspoon salt

1. Place all ingredients into the Vitamix container in the order listed and secure lid.

2. Select Variable 1.

3. Turn machine on and slowly increase speed to Variable 10, then to High.

4. Blend for 1 minute, using the tamper to press the ingredients into the blades.

5. Pour into saucepan and simmer for 20 to 30 minutes.

NOTE: This recipe is a great way to use up extra tomatoes; make 2 to 3 batches of sauce and freeze for later use.

Per 1/4 Cup (60 ml) Serving: 19 Cal (6% from Fat, 14% from Protein, 80% from Carb); 1 g Protein; 0 g Tot Fat; 0 g Sat Fat; 4 g Carb; 1 g Fiber; 3 g Sugar; 113 mg Sodium; 0 mg Cholesterol

puée

APPLESAUCE

preparation: 10 minutes • processing: 45 seconds • yield: 2 cups (480 g)

1-2 Tablespoons
lemon juice

4 medium apples,
1 1/2 pounds (724 g),
cored, quartered,
seeded with peel

1. Place all ingredients into the Vitamix container in the order listed and secure lid.

2. Select Variable 1.

3. Turn machine on and slowly increase speed to Variable 10, then to High.

4. Blend for 45 seconds, using the tamper to press the ingredients into the blades.

5. For chunky applesauce, blend on Variable 6 until desired consistency is reached.

NOTE: Use different varieties of apples to create your own signature applesauce. Add cinnamon or sugar if desired.

Per 1/2 Cup (120 g) Serving: 96 Cal (3% from Fat, 2% from Protein, 96% from Carb); 0 g Protein; 0 g Tot Fat; 0 g Sat Fat; 26 g Carb; 4 g Fiber; 19 g Sugar; 2 mg Sodium; 0 mg Cholesterol

purée

AVOCADO YOGURT SAUCE

preparation: 15 minutes • processing: 30 seconds • yield: 2 cups (480 ml)

3/4 cup (180 g) plain low fat yogurt

1 avocado, halved, pitted, peeled

1/2 garlic clove, peeled

1/2 lime, peeled

1/2 teaspoon salt

1/2 jalapeño pepper, 1 ounce (28 g), halved, seeds and membranes removed

2 Tablespoons (2 g) cilantro leaves

1. Place all ingredients into the Vitamix container in the order listed and secure lid.

2. Select Variable 1.

3. Turn machine on and slowly increase speed to Variable 10, then to High.

4. Blend for 30 seconds, using the tamper to press the ingredients into the blades

NOTE: Leave seeds and membranes in jalapeno for a spicier sauce. Serve with tacos, fajitas, seafood, and poultry or as a salsa alternative with chips.

Per 1/4 Cup (60 g) Serving: 51 Cal (56% from Fat, 13% from Protein, 31% from Carb); 2 g Protein; 3 g Tot Fat; 0 g Sat Fat; 4 g Carb; 2 g Fiber; 2 g Sugar; 167 mg Sodium; 0 mg Cholesterol

LOW FAT PUMPKIN PIE

preparation: 10 minutes • processing: 20-25 seconds • bake time: 1 hour
yield: 3 pies (24 slices)

1 cup (240 ml)
egg substitute

3 1/2 cups (850 g)
canned pumpkin

1 1/2 cups (300 g)
granulated sugar

1 teaspoon salt

2 teaspoons
ground cinnamon

1 teaspoon ground ginger

1/2 teaspoon
ground cloves

3 cups (720 ml)
evaporated nonfat milk

3 unbaked 9-inch (23 cm)
pie shells

whipped topping
(optional)

1. Preheat oven to 425°F (220°C).

2. Place egg substitute, pumpkin, sugar, salt, cinnamon, ginger, cloves, and evaporated milk into the Vitamix container in the order listed and secure lid.

3. Select Variable 1.

4. Turn machine on and slowly increase speed to Variable 10, then to High.

5. Blend for 20 to 25 seconds.

6. Pour into 3 unbaked 9-inch (23 cm) deep-dish pie shells.

7. Bake for 15 minutes. Reduce oven temperature to 350°F (180°C). Bake for 40 minutes. Pie is done when knife inserted into center comes out clean. Filling will be soft, but firms up as it sets and cools.

8. Chill and serve topped with whipped topping.

Per Slice (without whipped topping): 174 Cal (29% from Fat, 10% from Protein, 61% from Carb); 4 g Protein; 5 g Tot Fat; 1 g Sat Fat; 27 g Carb; 1 g Fiber; 19 g Sugar; 254 mg Sodium; 1 mg Cholesterol